A Woman's

Voice

~ Inspirational Short Stories ~

Volume 3

DOLORES AYOTTE

A Woman's Voice (Inspirational Short Stories) Volume 3
Copyright © 2014 by Dolores Ayotte. All rights reserved

No part of this publication may be reproduced, stored in a retrieval system or transmitted in any way by any means, electronic, mechanical, photocopy, recording or otherwise without the prior permission of the author except as provided by Canada and United States copyright law.

Book design copyright © 2014 by Dolores Ayotte. All rights reserved.
Cover design by Dolores Ayotte
Cover photo by Shirley Gauthier Sarafinchan
Interior design by Dolores Ayotte
Printed by CreateSpace
Published in Canada
ISBN: 978-0-9948673-3-9
Self-Help, Motivational & Inspirational

Disclaimer: The suggestions provided in this inspirational book are based on a personal point of view and not in any professional capacity.

The Human & Humane Self-Help Author

Dolores holds a Bachelor of Arts degree with a major in psychology from the University of Winnipeg as well as teacher certification from the University of Manitoba. She has also taken courses in human relationships and communication.

Her self-help books are written in retrospect based on a proven recipe, one she has incorporated step by step into her own life. Over time, Dolores eventually developed better life coping skills which inspired her to put pen to paper and write four other books about her experiences. She utilizes quotes, anecdotes, humor, and her own personal stories when necessary to make her suggestions relevant and to give an example of how to use her simple tips in daily living.

She is now retired and spends half the year with her husband at a retirement community in Arizona. For the remainder of the year, Dolores enjoys her children and grandchildren in Winnipeg, Manitoba where she was born and raised. She continues to learn from all the people who touch her life.

Table of Contents

Introduction
1. Old Black Thumb
2. These Boots
3. Peace in Life's Simple Pleasures
4. Two Wrongs
5. Genetics and Depression
6. My Oxygen Mask
7. Dysfunctional Mother/Daughter Relationships
8. Storage Bins
9. Taking Notice
10. The Three Faces of Eve
11. Spit It Out
12. On Being Tested
13. Objections Anyone…
14. The Weather Channel
15. Early Bird
16. Sadness
17. The Art of Playing Cards
18. The Persistence of the Spirit
19. Leadership
20. A New Word to Make you Smile

21	Driving Miss "D"
22	Change
23	Live…Laugh…Love
24	My Phantom Tooth
25	Common Courtesy
26	What's Eating Gilbert Grape
27	Self-Acceptance and Regrets
28	And the Winner is…Not Me!
29	Extraordinarily Ordinary
30	Savor the Flavor

Conclusion

Bonus Chapter ~ *From A Woman's Voice ~ Volume 2 ~ The Inception of A Woman's Voice*

Introduction

A Woman's Voice ~ Volume 3 is the last book in this three part series. I hope you enjoy reading this inspirational book as much as I've enjoyed writing it. Once again, I have included some guest writers who have agreed to share their thoughts with us. My daughter Andrea Cockerill has written several stories in Volumes 1 & 2 and is featured again in Volume 3. My husband Fred Ayotte is also featured in Volume 1 and now again in Volume 3. As usual, I have utilized numerous quotes and anecdotes from both women and men alike to add to your reading pleasure. I prefer to draw from a wide wealth of wisdom and enjoy the sagacity of both genders. I also recommend that you read all of my books in doses, not unlike taking medicine. These motivational writings are not meant to be read in one or two sittings like fictional books and perhaps like other non-fictional books. My books are meant to be digested in small doses in order to reflect upon and perhaps glean the guidance that we may need in order to better cope with the challenges of life. On the whole, the majority of the stories in Volume 3 are short and easy to read.

I would like to take this opportunity to thank Fred, Andrea, and Shirley for both their past and present contributions to the success of A Woman's Voice. As you can see by this lovely cover, a photo generously provided by my talented sister Shirley Gauthier Sarafinchan, the reflection in the water can be seen as a gentle reminder that as life goes on we have many opportunities to live, learn, and reflect on life in general. We also have every opportunity to learn from these reflections to help ensure that history doesn't repeat itself.

"Writing makes a person very vulnerable. It opens you to public criticism, to ridicule, to rejection. But it also opens conversation and thought. It stirs minds, and touches hearts. It brings us into contact with our souls. So how can it possibly be a waste of time, an idle act, a mistake, a betrayal of truth? Who can possibly tell us not to do it?" ~ *Joan Chittister, Order of Saint Benedict*

The above quote is very fitting and really hits home for me. It is found in the Introduction of A Woman's Voice ~ Volume 2 and is well worth repeating in Volume 3 as it applies to all my writing. I could not possibly express this message in my own words any better than Joan Chittister. At times, I feel the need to admit that I have also been discouraged. I, too, have felt vulnerable and affected by other people's views of me. Other times, I have been both criticized and rejected because of what I've shared. I've even had a few of my friends use what I have written to hurt me. When people have access to our innermost selves, this information can, at times, be used in unkind ways. Sharing our heart is similar to wearing our hearts on our sleeves...it leaves us wide open. As writers, we truly become open books. So why do we do it? I have the answer in a nutshell, at least from my point of reference. There is a niggling inside of us that just won't go away until we put pen to paper and write our thoughts and bare our souls. There is a deep thirst inside an author that will only be quenched by having or making the opportunity to express these inner seeds. They may start off so small but manage to grow into a book one day.

I repeat that I have known disappointment and discouragement but...I totally agree with this quote by Joan Chittister. My writing has stoked conversations outside of people's natural comfort zones. People have opened up to me and told me about their personal struggles because they know I understand and have compassion for their plight. My words have also stirred minds and touched hearts as I spur on people to think for themselves. I also encourage others to learn to love themselves in order to truly love, accept, and respect others. Believe me, this is no easy feat and not one I take lightly.

Yes…writing is no "idle act, no "mistake", and not meant to be "a betrayal of truth". At least, not my writing anyway. Writing is a gift that has been bestowed upon me and many others like me who want to share their talent with the world. To do less or to bury this talent would be a betrayal not only to myself but to My Maker and the One who so generously and abundantly gives us all a variety of gifts to share with our fellow humankind. Yes…sometimes it can hurt, but the rewards for our desire to share this wondrous gift usually far outweigh the negative consequences. Therefore, I salute all my fellow writers today. Chin up. Even if we positively touch only a few people with our written words, we have touched a whole world to God. I also salute those who take or make the time to read our words. Without them…we would be like a tree that falls in the forest with no one around to hear the sound of its impact. Yes indeed…as an author I have something to say. If you are an author reading my words, you know exactly what I mean. If you are a reader of inspirational books, you are honoring me beyond words by reading what is near and dear to my heart. Hopefully, what I have to share will touch your heart in a very intimate way.

"Courage is the price that life exacts for granting peace." ~ Amelia Earhart

1 ~ Old Black Thumb

"I have learned that success is measured not so much by the position one has reached in life as by the obstacles he has overcome." ~ Booker T. Washington

When I wrote my first book, **I'm Not Perfect And It's Okay ~ Steps to a Happier Self**, I quickly stated that I was "no author" in the introduction. Some people may find this a strange comment coming from a person who was in the processing of publishing a book.

At that time, my goal was to reach out to people to help prevent them from experiencing what I had been through with my bouts of serious depression. I was simply a greenhorn when it came to any kind of writing, so therefore, I didn't claim to be an author. I merely considered myself to be a person reaching out to help others. I wanted to touch as many lives as possible and I didn't know any other way except by the written word.

My gardening fame falls into much the same category. I'm "no gardener" but I sure have been trying all my life to be one. My husband can attest to this fact because he appears to be right there by my side. Although, he claims he is "no gardener" himself, the two of us persist in our endeavor to be the best at maintaining our backyard so it can be as picturesque as possible.

As the years have gone by, I know that at some point we crossed the line and can probably now call ourselves gardeners. The term old black thumb that my son-in-law first teasingly called me when he observed my lack of gardening skills, may no longer apply. He has now admitted that I'm actually better at it than he initially thought me to be. The proof is in the picture. I now have evidence to prove it.

I kind of feel the same way about my writing. I may have started off by stating that I was "no author" but with perseverance and dogged determination, I must admit I'm fast becoming one.

"I do not think there is any other quality so essential to success of any kind as the quality of perseverance. It overcomes almost anything, even nature." ~ John D. Rockefeller

Personal Reflections:

1. Do you have a hobby or engage in an activity that you know you could be better at?

2. Do you stick with it until you achieve a level of success that you are satisfied with or do you give up too soon? In other words, do you persevere in attaining a certain level of satisfaction?

3. Do you compare yourself to others or do you treat yourself as the unique individual that you are and make every effort to attain your own personal goals according to what you are capable of?

2 ~ These Boots

"The spirit, and the will to win, and the will to excel are the things that endure." ~ *Vince Lombardi*

Some of you may have already read the book I referred to in the previous chapter, therefore, I am not going to go into too much detail about the content. I just want to share with you one of the first small steps of many more steps to come that helped me turn my life around. In this motivational book, I state that it is very hard to motivate ourselves when we have little desire and even less energy to do so.

Many of us have been there. There is something inside us that tells us things just aren't quite right. We want to be right with ourselves and right with the world. There is an inner discontentment that sits in the pit of our stomach which affects our zest for life. It is extremely difficult to get past this malaise because we hate the way we feel about ourselves, our jobs, and many other aspects of our lives. We have no idea how to remedy the situation or where to start to get ourselves on a more positive track. In the end, we can actually hate ourselves because we don't or can't understand what is wrong with us. We may reach an all-time low and once we do, there is only one way to go and that is up.

I recommend this suggestion based on my own experiences. Start by one small step at a time…one small accomplishable step in the right direction. I started by actually taking physical steps by beginning a daily walking routine, one block of walking, day after day until I built myself up to three miles a day. That was over twenty-five years ago. It was the best decision I've ever made in helping myself get out of the pit I found myself to be in. I got off the bench in life and became a player. I took charge of my own life and decided to make a difference. It worked. I sang this song as I walked, "these boots are made for walking and"…that's just what I did! I had to help myself. There was no other way! My dad often used this expression, "The Good Lord helps those who help themselves!" It's very true. Just try it and you'll find out for yourself.

"The journey of a thousand miles begins with a single step." ~ Miyamoto Musashi

Personal Reflections:
1. Do you find yourself down in the dumps more often than you think is healthy for you?
2. Does this feeling of ennui trickle into other areas of your life?

3. Do you have a sense of peace or do you struggle with finding contentment in your life?
4. Do you agree that starting with one small easy step could help turn your life around?

3 ~ Peace in Life's Simple Pleasures

"For fast-acting relief try slowing down." ~ **Lily Tomlin**

So many people have touched my life in such a positive and inspirational way that I want to share some of their beliefs and ideas with as many people as possible. This is an example of one of life's simple pleasure.

A dear friend of mine sent me a very simple message not too long ago. *"How are you enjoying spring? I have been spending long days outdoors working in the yard and cleaning up the gardens for summer. I hear the birds singing and busily eating at the feeders, and wonder, who needs radios and cell phones when there is so much to enjoy in the natural world all around us? What peace there is in just melding into the world around you and doing ordinary things and realizing that...this is as good as it gets!"*

When I first received this little message, my imagination took me into my own garden and how I feel when I am there. In the spring, as I clean up my garden with the help of my husband, I feel the exact same way.

I get so lost in the wonder of it all that the work I am doing doesn't feel like work at all. I look in awe as I see the bushes and trees bud and turn green almost right before my eyes. I watch in amazement as I notice new growth sprout from the soil after a long cold winter. I gaze at the birds and listen with pleasure to their sweet songs as they go about their daily routine. I see the empty nests in our trees and bushes and I know a new season of life has begun.

I have a little garden sign in one of my flower beds which reads "Life Began in a Garden". Every time I read this sign, I am reminded of how close I am to Our Creator as I cultivate this little piece of earthly heaven that I call home.

"You must be the change you wish to see in the world." ~ Mahatma Gandhi

Personal Reflections:
1. Do you enjoy life's simple pleasures?
2. If so, which ones are they and how do you show your appreciation and gratitude for them?
3. Do you ever give any consideration to the adage "less is more" in order to take advantage of creating less stress in your life by merely taking more time to wake up and smell the roses?

4 ~ Two Wrongs

"There is no right way to do the wrong thing." ~ **Harold S. Kushner**

My dad used to have one of the neatest sayings. It's been over twenty years since he passed away. I still miss him and the impact he had on my life to this very day. He was not a well-educated man nor was he perfect. I certainly remember thinking he was when I was a young child. You know how little girls can idolize their fathers. Well, I was no exception. I had such an innocent love and high regard for him that I had him on a pretty high pedestal. It took me well into my adult years to fully realize that my dad was human just like the rest of us. I used to think he could do no wrong. I spent plenty of time listening to him and the stories he had to share. He also had quite a few cute sayings. One of them that has come to mind many times over the years is "two wrongs don't make a right". I'm sure he didn't coin this phrase but it sure felt like he did.

I can't count the number of times I heard him say this adage throughout my life. When people hurt us, we have the tendency to want to hurt them right back. There seems to be a trait in our human nature that likes to get even. As I write this, there is something that happened to me to make me think of these words of wisdom. Not all people are kind and it's very difficult to be kind to people who have shown unkindness toward us. Today is a day when I need to remind myself to be kind to these people. This is when I can hear my dad loud and clear, "two wrongs don't make a right". To be unkind toward someone who has hurt me will never make things right. I will be no further ahead than the person who was initially unkind to me. Yes…my dad may not have been the best educated man in the world nor was he perfect but just the same, he sure had plenty of wisdom.

It's neat how God works to get us the messages that we need to hear if we are in tune to His communication and open to this concept. Before I went to bed I wrote this little story because I was upset. I needed to remind myself to be kind no matter what. Drawing from my memory bank, I was able to hear my father once again remind me about acceptable behavior in order to better deal with those who may have hurt me. I guess we need to hear things more than once. At times, it is also beneficial to listen to the messages outside of our own thoughts and prayers. It may give us the clarity and vision that we are seeking. God works through people and by being open to their ideas and voices of wisdom, we can also find answers to our prayers and the inner peace we are striving to attain.

"The person who pays an ounce of principle for a pound of popularity gets badly cheated." ~ Ronald Reagan

Personal Reflections:
1. Do you take the time to analyze your situation or do you react too quickly?
2. Do you see yourself as trying to pay people back for their unacceptable behavior?
3. Do you agree with my dad that "two wrongs don't make a right" or do you desire to seek revenge for wrongdoings committed against you or yours?
4. If so, do you feel good about it when you've wronged the offenders liked they've wronged you? In other words, does it make you feel better or worse?

5 ~ Genetics and Depression

"Most of the important things in the world have been accomplished by people who have kept on trying when there seemed to be no hope at all." ~ Dale Carnegie

Over thirty six years ago I gave birth to twin daughters. I didn't even know I was having twins until the day I went into labor. You can well imagine our surprise as well as our delight. Our two-year old daughter was equally delighted with her two new baby sisters. Soon after I gave birth, many people asked me if twins ran in my family. I answered…"not to my knowledge". Shortly thereafter, I heard from extended family members that there were indeed many sets of twins on both sides of the family. I only discovered this fact later on in life because now this information had more relevance to my particular situation.

In several of my books, I've discussed the topic of depression. I have briefly touched on the premise that depression can be anger turned inward. Today, I am going to discuss another opinion I have about depression. I am not a medical professional. This is only a personal opinion based on my own experience with this debilitating condition.

Perhaps, you have already been exposed to the word "predisposition". This is the word I am going to use to elaborate on what I refer to as a genetic link to depression. We have already heard, when referring to the medical model, that certain physical illnesses are genetically linked like heart disease, cancer, high blood pressure, and so on. Due to this genetic link we might be more apt to get or inherit these diseases from our ancestors. I think that a similar analogy can also be made with other illnesses like depression. When I suffered my severe bout with depression in my early thirties, I had a better look as to why I had this illness when many of my peers did not. This realization was similar to when I gave birth to twins. I subsequently learned that many of my family members had also suffered or were still suffering from a range of mild to moderate and sometimes severe depression in a similar way to me. When this debilitating illness became more relevant to me, I had a better look. In doing so, I discovered that there seemed to be a genetic link to my illness because there was a long list of family members who shared my plight.

I came to the conclusion that one of my genetic weaknesses had to do with my family history of depression. I now refer to this as my "genetic predisposition" to this particular condition. To me, it is no different than any other genes that we might inherit. In my opinion, having this "predisposition" does not necessarily mean that we will suffer from depression or other forms of mental illness. What it does mean is that we might have the propensity to the perils of depression if a traumatic event occurs in our lives to "trigger" an episode. Such traumatic events may include the after effects of combat, the death of a loved one, divorce, job loss, financial woes, stress, etc. Some of these events are impossible to control and can have a devastating effect on those with a "predisposition" to depression.

According to depression expert, Nancy Schimelpfening in her article "Depression Causes" published in December, 2011..."*The causes of depression are not entirely understood, but are thought to be multi-factorial. Studies indicate that depression is, at least in part, an inherited condition involving abnormalities in neurotransmitter functioning. Although inheritance is an important factor in major depression, it does not account for all cases of depression, implying that environmental factors may either play an important causal role or exacerbate underlying genetic vulnerabilities.*"

In a perfect world where there are no traumatic events, possibly there would be no depression. I don't know. However, I do know that this is not a perfect world.

Although, we have no control over our genetic make-up, in a lot of instances we do have some control over the "triggers" that may cause our possible depression. From my personal frame of reference, this was what I have strived to achieve in overcoming my own depression. What I am basically saying here is this. If you suffer from symptoms of depression, the best course of action is to try to figure out what is causing it. This is the first step. After that, you may just succeed in figuring out what to do about it. If the "triggers" are within your power to control or avoid, your depression may also be managed more effectively if you make a conscious effort to avoid these situations whenever possible.

"When you reach the end of your rope, tie a knot in it and hang on." ~ *Thomas Jefferson*

Personal Reflections:

1. Do you have a genetic predisposition to depression or other forms of mental illness?
2. If so, do you take the necessary precautions to ensure that you protect yourself from possible triggers that will exacerbate your condition?
3. If you are aware of what the triggers are that negatively affect your condition, do you feel that it is

your personal responsibility to take care of yourself and prevent depressive episodes?

4. Do you agree that this is not an easy feat and that it might be necessary to seek professional help, reach out to a supportive loved one, or find a support group to help you avoid this negative life cycle?

6 ~ My Oxygen Mask

"Setting a goal is not the main thing. It is deciding how you will go about achieving it and staying with that plan." ~ Tom Landry

Not too long ago, I was listening to a talk show on the radio. I had turned on the radio expecting to hear music and instead there was a discussion going on about the joy found in being a Christian. My ears perked up and I couldn't help but listen more carefully as the guest speaker described what he thought it was like to be a Christian. He went on to say that God is supposed to come first in our lives which, by the way I fully agree with, family and friends are supposed to come second…and then we as individuals are supposed to come third. He then stated that we have been put on this earth to serve others.

Based on my religious education I know that some people may believe this to be true but I also know that it is a hard ideal to live up to. I want to be realistic about myself as a human being. I know that with all my human weaknesses and frailties, I am not always able to put others before myself and my own needs each and every time. I have also come to realize that this teaching is not always meant to be so cut and dry and by putting myself last, I may not be obeying what God has in store for me as one of His followers.

I remember working with a gentleman who told me a story as he watched me trying to adhere to the rule of serving others. I wasn't even aware that he was observing me in this way. One day while discussing business in his office, he reminded me of the oxygen masks on airplanes and how to properly use them. He was a fellow Christian and he felt the need to reinforce the fact that I was supposed to put on my own oxygen mask first before I rushed around to help others. I still find it interesting to this day that he chose to share this bit of advice with me. Whatever he was observing about my behavior at work, he obviously felt the need to step in and give me a little fatherly advice. I must admit that it was good advice and I took it in the way that it was intended.

I learned from him that it is perfectly okay to first take care of my own needs in certain instances in order to better see to others and their needs. Not everything said or read is so black and white. This gentleman took the time to educate me because he felt it was necessary to do so. For whatever reason, he thought I was risking my own health in order to serve others. He stepped outside of his comfort zone to explain this concept to me. I thanked him for steering me in the right direction. By using this analogy, I figuratively learned to first put on my own oxygen mask in life in order to make sure I was there for the long haul. In doing so, I could better serve others according to God's Plan and not my own.

At times, it is not only appropriate but very necessary to put our needs ahead of others to ensure that we can actually serve God in the way that we were meant to serve. This man served me that day and I have learned to serve others in much the same way. If I don't have my oxygen mask on, I'm not going to last very long and I won't be of any use at all.

"The highest reward for a person's toil is not what he gets for it, but what he becomes by it." ~ *John Ruskin*

Personal Reflections:

1. Do you agree with the advice given to me by the gentleman in this story?
2. If so, do you take the necessary precautions to protect yourself so that you will have the staying power to stand the test of time?
3. If not, do you see yourself as the kind of person that must always come last? If so, why?
4. For those of you who think that you should come last in order to serve God, are you certain this is God's

will for you? At times, it is very difficult to discern the difference between our will and the image we want to project and what God's will actually is for us. This effort requires much prayer, discernment, and open-mindedness.

7 ~ Dysfunctional Mother/Daughter Relationships

"Within our dreams and aspirations we find our opportunities." ~ Sue Atchley Ebaugh

Over the Christmas Season, I had the opportunity to enjoy a few movies. For several days, both my husband and I were struggling with the flu and colds. It was a great opportunity to find some enjoyment during the recuperating period by watching movies on TV. My husband went to bed earlier than usual one evening because he was feeling so under the weather. While I was channel hopping I came across a movie that was already in progress. It was a simple, little movie that would appeal to all age groups but probably more to children than to adults.

It was the story about two mothers who were extremely different. One was a teacher who was very concerned about the education of her teenage daughter. Her main desire was to see her daughter excel academically and to get accepted into Harvard. The other mother was an ice skating coach. She, on the other hand, wanted her daughter to excel at ice skating and perhaps qualify for the Olympics. As you have probably already guessed, it was as if each of these mothers had given birth to the wrong daughter. The daughter with the academic mother was a gifted skater and it was her dream to be an Olympic champion. The daughter of the ice skating coach wasn't at all interested in following in her mother's footsteps. She wanted to excel academically.

Both mothers refused to look at what their daughters aspired to be and only looked at what they wanted for their daughters. They both thought that they knew best and were extremely adamant about it. The academic mother went so far as to refuse to even go watch her daughter skate. She was totally unaware of how gifted her daughter was in this area. She was very closed-minded. In essence, both these mothers were living vicariously through their daughters. They actually wanted their daughters to succeed where they had failed. They were both so controlling in trying to accomplish their own end goals.

How many of us are just like that? We have our own agenda and we look at what we want without giving any thought to what anyone else wants.

It doesn't necessarily have to be in a dysfunctional mother/daughter relationship. This lack of communication and unattractive power struggle can be found in any relationship. Balance...equality...mutual respect. These may appear to be lofty goals but with honesty, desire, and hard work, they are definitely attainable and well worth the effort.

"You will become as small as your controlling desire, as great as your dominant aspiration." ~ James Allen

Personal Reflections:
1. Are we really looking at the people in our lives from their point of view? This is no easy task. What do you think?
2. Do you feel that you must suppress whom you really are in order to stay in a relationship or do you feel the need to be in charge because you are insecure or threatened by those around you?
3. If things don't go your way, do you try to accept the situation in a mature way or do you lash out?

8 ~ Storage Bins

"We do not remember days, we remember moments."
~ Pavese, Cesar

Life is like a closet full of clothes. It's very difficult to know what you want to give away, donate, or discard. It's even harder to discard some of those items that have been given to you as gifts or those that have sentimental value. Some of these items may have little or no monetary worth but they fill our drawers and our storage bins. I have many such items that I cannot part with because they mean so much to me.

If I keep these items, will they have any special meaning to my children or my grandchildren? The last birthday card signed "with love" by my mother-in-law before she died over twenty years ago, the ripped sheet of paper from an old prayer-book with my father's signature so proudly written on it, the scribbled notes that my granddaughter left in the bathroom cupboard, the popcorn pictures and artwork from my other grandchildren, and the albums of numerous pictures that my husband has so conscientiously organized...who will want these treasures that I have saved?

When I was seventeen years old, my then boyfriend was chosen to go on a school trip to Vancouver, BC. On his return, he gave me a beautiful sweater. That was almost fifty years ago. That boyfriend became my husband, my friend, my lover, my confidant. Who will want that "holey" not "holy" sweater I have so carefully wrapped and stored in some box in my basement? Our children are going to have a huge laugh on us one day as they sort through our belongings and discover how sentimental we are.

To continue in this vein, when I was a very young girl my father gave me a blunt-ended little hammer. One morning as I was walking with my girlfriends, we started to discuss how sentimental we've all become as we age. We've discovered that keepsakes actually matter much more to us now than they did in our youth.

One friend was explaining this fact by sharing a story with us. She said she went through a lot of work and effort to make small quilts that she gave as presents to her children and grandchildren. After they were used for their initial purpose and as the years went by, they were eventually used in some other constructive way. The other way she noticed was that they ended up at the bottom of the dog kennel. By the pained expression on her face, it seemed to me that she would have preferred that her children were more sentimental. It was also apparent to me that she hoped they would cherish these homemade quilts in much the same way that they were created...with love. Perhaps in her children's opinion they were cherished because they did indeed love their dogs.

I then took this opportunity to share my story about my handy little hammer with my friends. It goes like this. Many years ago when I was a preschooler and several times thereafter, I used to work in the garage with my Dad. He was a self-taught carpenter as well as a general handy man. I loved to spend time with him in whatever way possible. During one of these special times, he gave me a small hammer to call my own. Over the years, I didn't think too much about that hammer but when I got married over forty-five years ago and left home, my Dad gave it to me.

A couple of months ago, one of my granddaughters phoned and asked if she could spend the day with us. I quickly agreed to this request. Her dad was on his way out and he promptly dropped her off at our house. Grandpa was busy hanging pictures using my cherished little hammer so I asked our granddaughter to hand the hammer to grandpa when he needed it. I then explained to my six-year-old granddaughter that I used this very hammer when I was about her age. She looked at me with that quizzical look of hers and asked "really". I'm sure she wondered if I was ever really that young.

I proceeded to tell her how precious this hammer was to me because it was a gift from my father. I further added that one day I would love to give it to her but I wanted to wait until she could realize the importance of it. I definitely want to pass my hammer along. Even as simple and as old as this gift may be, I want her to keep it and do the same. Now isn't that silly? Well not "really", at least not to me. My hammer signifies a lovely memory and a cherished part of my life. The words that I write have much the same meaning. My words are my hammer. It's why I write. I want my words to be passed along down the line to all who are willing to read them. I have a message. My message means an awful lot to me. In my early thirties I dreamed of writing a book to share my message. After twenty-five years of dreaming, I finally got started and haven't stopped since.

"You are never too old to set another goal or dream a new dream." ~ C.S. Lewis

Personal Reflections:

1. Do you have a message or any special mementoes that you would like to keep in your family?

2. Do you consider yourself to be a sentimental person?
3. Have you become more sentimental with age?
4. Does anyone else share in your sentimental pleasure of simple things?
5. Do you struggle with parting with these items? If so, in my opinion, that's a good thing. Trust me, you are not alone.

9 ~ Taking Notice

"Life is either a daring adventure or nothing." ~
Helen Keller

Once and awhile I am inspired to veer off in another direction. I see this as a chance to either lighten up or to inject a little variety into my stories by looking at things from a different angle. As you've probably already gathered, I am a thinker. When I published my first book, my editor sent me a little message. She suggested that I write more and think less. I tried my best to comply. It was not an easy request for me. I have to admit that I do a lot of meditating especially in the wee hours of the morning. I also do my fair share of reflecting and analyzing life and the challenges it poses. Oftentimes, I also find great pleasure and entertainment in people watching or observing simple human behavior. One of these occasions has prompted me to ask the following questions.

When people take group pictures and show you the results, whose face do you look for when viewing the developed product? When there is some kind of contest or game that you have subscribed to and a list of winners is provided, who do you look for in the slate of names? When you make a subtle change with your appearance or lifestyle do you expect people to notice? When you speak, do you expect people to listen?

All these questions…where could I possibly be going with this? Well, if you are anything like me, these questions were quite simple to answer. I am no different than any one of you. When I know I'm in a photo, I zoom into the picture of me to see how I look. When winners or names are announced or posted, I immediately look to see where I stand. When I change my appearance or wear something new, I hope somebody will notice and perhaps make a comment or compliment me on the change. I definitely appreciate when my friends and family listen to what I have to say and show an interest in the topic or news that I am sharing with them.

After admitting this not only to myself but to my readers as well, I then proceed to go one step further. I frequently ask myself if I do the same for others in much the same way that I hope or expect them to do for me. I feel it is necessary to remind myself that I can't ask a desired behavior from others if I am not prepared to deliver it myself. Plain and simple, in order to look at and listen to others more effectively, we must make a conscious decision to offer this same consideration.

Therefore, I can merely ask one more question. Are you taking the time to really notice someone or something about another person other than focusing on yourself? If you are, this is what relationship building is all about.

The title of this little chapter **Taking Notice** reminds me of an incident that took place in a social function some time ago. I am what most people would consider to be the average Joe. I am very down to earth and I pretty well blend in wherever I go. I am not the kind of person that stands out and for all intents and purposes, I am not comfortable with being the center of attention. In a very small group of four to six people, I can be seen as the life of the party but in a larger group I seem to fade away. In other words, I'm far more an introvert than an extrovert.

Many years ago I attended a large staff Christmas party with my husband. Actually it was his staff party and I knew very few people which I admit, contributed to my awkwardness in this type of situation. The wife of one of my husband's co-workers came up to me later on in the evening and made a comment to me that I have never forgotten.

She said, *"You are the type of person that no one would ever notice when they first walked into a room. However, if they took the time to take a second look, they would never forget you".*

I hardly knew this woman, yet her words had a profound effect on me. At first blush, as already mentioned, I'm an average looking person. Also, as I said before, I really don't stand out in any way, shape or form. I seldom draw attention to myself by anything I say, do, or wear in these types of situations. In fact, I will usually go out of my way to avoid the limelight in these large group settings.

What this woman said to me was a two-sided comment. I sensed that she meant it as a compliment and chose to see the bright side and learn from her words. How many people appear to be just like the average Joe? If or when we take the time to have a second look and draw them out, we may be very pleasantly surprised by what we discover.

Some people are very comfortable with being in the center of things and have no trouble drawing attention to themselves. In fact, it is very natural for them to do so. For those that aren't nearly as comfortable, it's a great idea for us to take the time to have a second look and see what we might have missed the first time around.

I'm grateful to that woman who managed to teach me this very simple yet valuable lesson. I have been taking a second look at the people around me ever since. It has paid off big time and I have discovered many diamonds in the rough.

"Give the world the best that you have, and the best will come back to you." ~ Madeline Bridges"

Personal Reflections:

1. Do you like being the center of attention?
2. Would you consider yourself to be an introvert or an extrovert?
3. Do you take the time to truly notice those around you and give them more than a passing glance?
4. Do you agree that we might miss some very meaningful friendships by not taking a second look?

10 ~ The Three Faces of Eve

"Never mistake knowledge for wisdom. One helps you make a living; the other helps you make a life." ~ Sandra Carey

Over fifteen years ago, due to a job change by my husband, we decided to move to a small town. It had a population of about 900 people and was situated about a two-hour drive from the large city which had been our home for most of our lives. At this time, our three daughters were not yet married, although one was already on her own. The other two, our nineteen year old twins, were full-time university students still living at home. I was working full-time at a major financial institution. From my point of view, this was what I considered to be a major lifestyle change. We found an apartment for the girls, sold our house, quit our jobs, and moved to this quaint little town. We lived there for six years.

On looking back, I don't know how we did it. It had a huge impact on all of us. Our girls found their independence after the usual trials and tribulations. My husband settled into his job and I did the best I could to fill the void in my life. This was the first time in several years that I didn't work outside the home. I became involved in a variety of volunteer projects in order to amuse myself and fill my now long days.

One of the things I decided to do, was to take a few painting classes. I did not have an artistic bone in my body up to this point and I had no idea what to expect. I bought my supplies and proceeded to try to learn how to be an artist. I didn't go to many classes, but I still persisted in painting on my own. During the six-year period in this small town, I painted numerous pictures. Once we moved back to the big city just over fifteen years ago, I never painted again.

When living in Pine Falls, my husband used to tease me and say that I was one of the most prolific painters he had ever seen. During this six-year period, I probably painted thirty-five pictures. I never sold one painting, although, a few people were gracious enough to accept the odd gift. Most paintings were "the pits" even from my own standards but there are a few that I cherish. Three of them remain very special to me even to this day and I have them hanging in our home.

This first painting is picture of a young girl about the age of eight years old. She is very sad and she symbolizes a "sorrowful child". The second picture is also of a young girl. She is probably in her early teens and of Amish descent. From the outside, you can see that there is no physical relationship between the two girls. I refer to this girl as a "shy youth". The third painting is that of an older native woman and once again appears to bear no relationship to the other two paintings. I call this painting a "wiser older woman". She represents what I consider myself to be similar to today as I am an older woman compared to the first two young girls. It has taken many years and many personal trials and tribulations to arrive at this point in my life.

I call these combined portraits, "The Three Faces of Eve" because they show the distinct facets and faces of my own personality and the stages I have gone through to become who I am today. I am not alone. Each of us has many different facets to our personalities. These three distinct faces demonstrate my own personal growth. They are actually an x-ray view of myself. I have used a unique and creative way to paint a self-portrait. I have chosen to paint myself from the inside out to demonstrate my maturation process.

We all have hidden talents. It took me a long time to realize what some of mine might be. True growth is discovering whom we really are and having both the courage and the freedom to express it. This experience has been very liberating for me and one I have learned to truly appreciate.

"History has demonstrated that the most notable winners usually encountered heartbreaking obstacles before they triumphed." ~ B.C. Forbes

Personal Reflections:

1. Have you had a good look at yourself lately?
2. Are you tapping into your creative abilities?
3. What does your x-ray (innermost self) look like? Our outside image or persona may be very different from our x-ray view.
4. Are you being true to yourself or do you hide behind a false image or facade?
5. Have you dared to remove your mask and truly be who you were meant to be?

11 ~ Spit It Out

"Love is everything. It is the key to life, and its influences are those that move the world." ~ Ralph Waldo Trine

My husband of over forty-five years is a pretty silent man. I married my high school sweetheart. No, we weren't the prom king and queen. As a matter of fact, he actually got chosen and I didn't. He was so gallant that he refused to accept this honor because he didn't want someone else by his side to share in this momentous teenage moment.

It's seems like a lifetime ago that we were playing the dating game in our eleventh grade classroom. My then boyfriend grabbed my attention right at the onset. Boy...he was one quiet guy and I sure made up for his silence when we were together.

Not too long ago, I had the sneaking suspicion that I said something to offend him. I wasn't a hundred percent sure because we were just heading off to bed after a late night with friends, but come morning there was no doubt about it.

By now you are probably asking yourself "how does a silent man tell you that you have offended him?" Body language, that's how!

When "Silent Sam" woke up at his usual time, I had been up and at it for about three hours. He got his usual cup of coffee and sat in his rocking chair across from me. That's not out of the ordinary. He gets up, gets his coffee, sits in silence and waits for me to say something to start our day.

Something was subtlety different this morning and a less experienced eye might have missed it. He did all the above mentioned things but in addition to these, he crossed his arms and then I knew for sure that I had offended him. He seldom crosses his arms first thing in the morning.

I knew he had "a burr in his saddle" and I suggested he "spit it out" so that we could get on with our day. That's exactly what he did after a little prodding from me. We then discussed what was bothering him and he got it off his chest. I've learned that it's best not to let things fester. It's far better to "spit it out" and then get on with life. Life's much too short to harbor resentment. Don't you think that it's much better to clear the air and move on?

Now, over forty-five years later, he is a little more talkative and I am a lot less than I was in our youth. Although, I still can outdo my husband, I have nowhere near as much to say these days. I find that we have long moments of silence in our home and it's not one bit awkward. We've discovered that we can still be in each other's company and provide a sense of comfort with silence. I like it and so does he. The pressure to fill the silence has been removed a long time ago as we embrace each other in this wonderful and pleasant way.

Yes...silence is okay too. In fact, in most instances I have come to cherish it and my husband is okay with it too. I may not have been chosen to be prom queen but my husband has done his best to treat me like royalty whenever possible. He can still be gallant these days too.

"Harmony is one phase of the great law whose spiritual expression is love." ~ James Allen

"A true friend is one who is concerned about what we are becoming, who sees beyond the present relationship, and who cares deeply about us as a whole person." ~ Gloria Gaither

Personal Reflections:

1. When a problem arises in any of your relationships, do you address it as soon as possible?
2. Do you agree that this is the wisest course of action?
3. Have you noticed that if you don't, the problem can morph into an even bigger one?

4. Do you manage to keep calm when facing a problematic situation or do you let anger get the best of you?

5. Do you ever go to bed angry or do you try your best to get over unpleasant situations so that they don't affect your emotional wellbeing?

12 ~ On Being Tested ~ Fred Ayotte

Now a few words of wisdom from my husband...

Many times in life we are tested by people in order to see if they can get a reaction out of us. We have all met someone who makes a comment or behaves in a way that is out of the norm. They are waiting to see how we will respond. If we are smart enough to realize what they are doing, we can really have fun by responding in a totally different way than they might expect. It is as if we've turned the table around and now their reaction to our unexpected response is sometimes worth the price. Two people can play the same game, don't you think?

This theory often holds true when teenagers interact with parents. I have been blessed with three beautiful daughters. When my oldest daughter was growing up everything was new to me as a parent. So as a father, I may have over reacted to certain behaviors based on my lack of experience. However, when my twins came along, I had learned to take things in better stride. One of my twin daughters who is now a beautiful, kind, and sensitive woman, went through a rebellious stage in her teens.

She had long beautiful hair which enhanced her good looks. I remember one day she came home from school and announced to her mother and me that she was shaving her head. She was about fifteen years old at the time and she wanted to make a statement...true beauty is on the inside of a person and she wanted to be regarded as a beautiful person. In other words, she had every desire for people to look at her kind and compassionate personality. My wife was very upset. I told her not to worry because the act of our daughter shaving her head was far better than a lot of other things that she could possibly be doing.

I remember vividly the night she came home with her hair all cut off. My wife had gone to bed and I was sitting in the living room. I think my daughter expected me to react to the bald look. All I did was go up to her, rub her head and say "hmmm fuzzy" and walk away. I don't know what reaction she expected to get from me but none was given other than this warm gesture. It wasn't too long after that, her hair grew back and we went on to the next issue.

Please note: The questions I am about to ask are created by me, not my husband.

Personal Reflections:

1. If there is one thing I learned from my husband in the previous situation...it is to not sweat the small stuff. Do you do just that?
2. Do you work yourself up over trivial things only to realize later on that it was no big deal?
3. Do you know how to put things into perspective in order to be more reasonable and less emotional when a problematic situation arises?

13 ~ Objections Anyone...

"Life is either a daring adventure or nothing. To keep our faces toward change and behave like free spirits in the presence of fate...is strength undefeatable." ~ Helen Keller

When I was graduating from high school, it seemed that there weren't many career choices for me. I'm not so sure if it was the fact that I was a female or if it had to do more with my financial situation or merely just plain lack of opportunity. Perhaps, it was a combination of all three.

In my nuclear family, it was far more the exception to get a university degree than it was the rule. Out of six children, only two of us attended university. I am sure the rest of my siblings would have enjoyed attaining a higher education as it certainly wasn't their lack of intelligence that kept them away...only a lack of opportunity and more than likely a lack of financial resources. A university degree was not easy to attain especially in my situation. I only managed to receive my degree on a part-time basis after I got married and while raising my young family.

Upon graduating from high school, it seemed that the majority of females, although not all, chose some kind of secretarial work, teaching, or nursing career. I was no different. A one year teacher certification program was being offered for free due to the shortage of teachers in our province. I jumped at the chance. I then proceeded to further educate myself at my own financial expense.

When I look at my high school year book, under my picture is the caption, Dolores "wants to be a lawyer...objections anyone?" As I recall that comment, I smile to myself. Today, I know for certain I am a teacher but I must admit, there is still something inside of me that is every bit the lawyer. I don't mean when it comes to matters of law, as much as the desire to "defend" a person who is being slandered or to "defend" a worthy cause. I figure we can have all kinds of "callings" without an official designation. What do you think? I am sure that I am not the only one that chose a different career option due to circumstance whether personal or financial. Perhaps like me, circumstances prevented you from fulfilling your initial dream or aspiration but maybe you've figured out how to feel rewarded nonetheless.

"The golden opportunity you are seeking is in yourself. It is not in your environment; it is not in luck or chance, or the help of others; it is in yourself alone." ~ Orison Swett Marden

Personal Reflections:

1. If you have a calling that is yet to be realized, what is it?
2. Is there still a chance that you might have another career or do you consider it to be too late?
3. If you were unable to follow your heart for whatever reason in your younger years, have you found a creative way to incorporate your initial career aspiration into your life in order to feel more fulfilled?

14 ~ The Weather Channel ~ On a Lighter Note

A little humor can go a long way...

Sometimes in life I feel like I am a cross between Erma Bombeck with her wry sense of humor and Phyllis Diller and her silliness about her husband, Fang. To quote Phyllis, she states that "his fine hour lasted about a minute and a half." I sincerely hope that some of you know who these two admirable women are even though Erma has now left her legacy with us and Phyllis is still hanging in there. I love both these women because they have such delightful senses of humor and they have succeeded in making a lot of people laugh over the years.

How great is that when you can bring a smile to someone's face, or light up their eyes with mirth, or get a burst of laughter that seems to come from the tips of their toes? Oh...to bring such pleasure and joy to other human beings. What a wonderful goal to strive for and to emulate. My desire to be similar to either of these two well-known women is quite the aspiration.

When a couple retires, they get a good taste at developing the kind of sense of humor it truly takes to sustain a long time marriage and ride off into the sunset together. During these retirement years, you have the opportunity to discover what your marriage vows are all about and what it really means to say "I do". When there is no one else to look at, you have plenty of time to have a better look at your lifelong partner. Some don't make it after almost a life time together. Just take a look at Al Gore and his wife Tipper. After forty years of marriage they bid each other adieu, even after that big smooch we observed on national television just a few short years ago.

One of the initial signs of being true retirees is when you have the Weather Channel on TV tuned in for several hours during the day. Your love is tested when you ask your husband what kind of weather to expect and he looks at you, points to his forehead and asks, "Do you see a weathervane on my forehead?" I cannot tell you how many times I've had that response when I ask my husband what it is like outside before I dress for our daily walk. In other words, do I need a jacket or don't I?

Hey, it could be worse. I could have to look at the Weather Channel myself. I much prefer to delegate this small task to my husband instead. You just can't help but love this guy. He's a real stand-up kind of fellow but sometimes I think he should be a sit-down-comedian as he shoots out his humorous commentary from his rocking chair in the den. Perhaps he is trying to emulate Jack Benny. He never ceases to amaze me with his one liners. He probably wouldn't mind using one of Jack's famous quotes right about now. Jack has been known to say, *"My wife Mary and I have been married forty-seven years, and not once have we had an argument serious enough to consider divorce…murder, yes…divorce, never."*

My husband really does watch the Weather Channel but he insists he's listening to the music. What do you think?

Here's another peek at the life of a longtime married couple just to give a heads up of what you have to look forward to if you haven't been married as long we have. A few years ago, my husband had double cataract surgery. His vision could no longer be corrected adequately enough with eyeglasses so it was recommended that he get new lenses. My husband has worn thick glasses ever since he was a young boy. As a result of the surgery, he ended up with extremely good distant vision. He now has 20/20 vision when seeing far away.

On the way home from the eye doctor after removal of the first patch, I could have sworn he was winking at me. He kept opening and closing his eye because he couldn't believe the difference in his vision. The colors were so bright. He repeatedly placed his hand on-and-off his good eye in his state of disbelief at what he could now see. Good thing I was driving, which is unusual in itself, but his now improved vision was equally unusual and he was extremely impressed with the results.

After his second eye surgery, he got his eyes retested and the prescription he received was for glasses that would accommodate his now, no-so-good "near" vision, a common side effect of cataract surgery. However, there was no way that this man was going to wear glasses...not after wearing them almost his entire life. He felt certain that he didn't need to wear glasses anymore. He then decided he could make do with glasses from the dollar store in order to read instead of getting the prescription that the eye doctor recommended.

Well, let me tell you, if we don't have ten pairs of glasses lying all around the house, we don't have one. They are on or in every nook and cranny you can imagine. Every time I talk to my husband when he's reading the newspaper, he peers over the top of his glasses at me. He needs glasses to read but to not see me across the room. I must admit, he looks quite professorial. I think God played a little trick on me. Now I am an older woman and my husband can see me even better than he did in his youth. Does that sound fair to you? Good thing he has some tact.

Personal Reflections:

1. Do you use humor in your life as often as possible?
2. Are you in a long term relationship? If so, can you relate to the need for a sense of humor?
3. Do you ever take a moment to really laugh with your partner or anyone else for that matter?

15 ~ Early Bird ~ More on a Lighter Note

"A bird doesn't sing because it has an answer, it sings because it has a song." ~ Maya Angelou

Is it true? Does the early bird really catch the worm? Every morning, it's the very same thing. No matter what time I go to bed at night, my internal clock wakes me up at about 5:00 am. In a sense, I should be annoyed and grumpy because a part of me would like to sleep in like other non-morning people. The other part of me loves this alone time.

I cannot tell you how productive I am first thing in the morning. I have anywhere between two to three hours before my husband saunters into the den with his morning cup of coffee. I kind of feel sorry for him because after several hours of quiet, albeit productive time, I am ready to talk to someone.

He's the only someone around and I'm sure, at times, he would like to press my off button this early in the morning. Trust me, it is already late from my frame of reference and I am eager to get started on the rest of my day.

I must admit that I have to back off just a little so that my husband can have a few moments of relaxation to enjoy his cup of coffee and newspaper first thing in the morning. He has the same right to do so even if it is almost three hours later than me. Hey, different personalities...it's what keeps us challenged as we learn to respect each other's differences.

I have the sneaking suspicion that early birds can get on some people's nerves now and then. I'm sure I rub my husband the wrong way occasionally. I realize that I can get on his only nerve with my morning chatter, but what the heck! We're two older birds in this empty nest of ours and we can enjoy life the way we see fit. We know how to work it out.

Yes...I'm a morning person. There's no getting around that fact. Most mornings I'm up before the crack of dawn, even before the sun pops up.

I can hardly ever remember getting up on the wrong side of the bed. Morning people are an odd bunch. Usually we can hardly wait to start the day and I'm no exception. I vividly recall one such memory that took place many years ago on the way to work with my husband. As I was humming along to a song, he suggested that if I was going to "chirp" all the way to work at 7:00 in the morning, I might have to consider taking a bus. Ouch!

Yes...my husband is the exact opposite. At times, he gives new meaning to the term grumpy first thing in the morning. As the day progresses, his face eventually lights up and so does his mood. By evening I can hardly recognize his sunny nature as my day starts to wind down. When they say that opposites attract, we certainly prove it in this area of our marriage.

My day coach turns back into a pumpkin long before midnight and certainly long before the big guy, as I lovingly refer to him, hits the sack.

My dad used to say, "It takes all kinds to make the world go around". How true. We're comparable to eggs. I'm sunny side up and my husband is scrambled. I'm relieved to say that he is definitely not hard-boiled. I like it that way. It provides for variety in our lives as it challenges us to learn how to respect each other's differences. It has been said that "variety is the spice of life". I know this to be true and I have a sneaking suspicion you do too.

"Personal relationships are the fertile soil from which all advancement, all success, all achievement in real life grows." ~ Ben Stein

Personal Reflections:

1. Are you an early bird or a late riser?

2. Who do you think is easier to live with or to be?
3. Do you adjust your schedule to accommodate your partner or is it the other way around?
4. If you both have the same time schedule, do you ever crave alone time at either the beginning or end of the day?

16 ~ Sadness

Sometimes, I also feel an overwhelming sense of sadness. My initial reaction is to try to push it away. I find it difficult to dwell in this experience. I then realize that if I sit in this moment and think through what is causing the sadness, I learn to make more sense of it.

Perhaps I have every reason to be sad upon hearing that my good friend has been diagnosed with cancer or that someone I love is going through a difficult time. It is okay for me to accept and embrace this sadness as I work through the pain of what others are experiencing. It is not necessary for me to push it away. It is only necessary for me to pray for these people and know that the moment will pass.

Sadly to say, it may take a long time for their moment to pass, so the least I can do is share in their suffering by not only being sad for them but by praying for them as well.

Personal Reflections:
1. Do you ever feel sad?
2. If so, why? Just know, it's okay to feel all of our emotions.

17 ~ The Art of Playing Cards ~ Fred Ayotte ~ More on a Lighter Note

Written by my husband...

"I love the winning, I can take the losing, but most of all I love to play the game." ~ Boris Becker

I grew up in a household where card playing was a family tradition. From an early age, I learned how to play children's games such as War, Go Fish, and Old Maid. As I grew older, my parents taught me how to play Hearts, Barouche, Cribbage, and more advanced card games. Therefore, as my daughters were growing up, carrying on this long time family tradition of playing cards came naturally.

When they were very young, one of their favorite games was Go Fish. We would literally play for hours. As much as I loved playing this game with them, I would get quite tired after a while especially after a long day at work. However, they never wanted to quit.

As you know, the game of Go Fish is about the matching of cards. You start by asking the other player if they have a certain card. If the answer is yes, they must give it to you. If not, then you just pick one from the deck. After hours of playing, if my young daughters didn't have the card I asked for, I eventually would pick one from the deck. I then put it in my matched cards pile whether they were a pair or not. Soon afterwards, the game would end. Nobody could figure out why they ended up with unmatched cards in their hands. I know some of you may call this cheating...I called it relief. It was time for the game to finally be over and for them to go to bed so that I could have a bit of an evening with my wife.

It wasn't until many years later that my daughters put two-and-two together and figured out what I had been up to so many years earlier. We all had a good laugh about it. What I didn't realize was that my oldest granddaughter Abby, who was about five at the time, was listening. She is now eighteen.

A few years later during one of our many visits to spend time with our eldest daughter and her family, Abby wanted us to play cards with her and her younger sister. They wanted to play Go Fish to be exact. Abby who was then eight years old was organizing the seating. She was telling her mother and grandmother where to sit as well as her younger sister Becca who was five. Becca is now fifteen. After Abby got everyone seated to her satisfaction, she looked right at me in a very serious demeanor and said "Grandpa, you sit beside me. I want to keep my eye on you because I hear you cheat at Go Fish". My wife and daughter just burst out laughing.

Alas, my reputation had caught up to me after all these years. Everyone had a good laugh and no one has let me forget it since.

Little ears…they hear everything! Are you setting a good example for your children and grandchildren?

18 ~ The Persistence of the Spirit
~ Andrea Ayotte Cockerill

Written by my daughter…

"What lies behind us and what lies before us are tiny matters compared to what lies within us." ~ Oliver Wendell Holmes

If you have ever been around children, you know how persistent they can be when they want your attention. All of my children let me know in their own way if they feel like they are not getting their fair share of my time. Today it was my oldest daughter who told me loud and clear that her well for my attention was running low.

After filling my daughter's desire for personal attention, I started thinking about how persistent our spirit can be when we are ignoring its guidance and passions. I have on many occasions put my spirit last on the list because I am comforted with the fact that my spirit is going nowhere. No matter how long I ignore it…it is like a patient and trusted friend, waiting for my next phone call.

Our relationship with our spirit is like any other relationship that we honor in our lives. It needs our time in order for an intimate bond to be built. It is the difference between talking to one friend every few months and talking to another friend every few days. You may cherish both friends but it is the friend whom you talk to more often that is going to know the more intimate details of your daily life. This same principle applies to our spirit. If we form an intimate relationship with our spirit, we will be better able to understand and intuitively follow its subtle guidance system.

Your spirit promises you that it will never reject you. It is persistent but patient, and its sole goal is to lead you to the Divine. Forming a relationship with your spirit needs to be a conscious decision on a daily basis, but the rewards span a life time.

Namaste ~ I see the Divine in you which is also in me.

"Continuous effort is the key to unlocking our potential." ~ *Black Elk, Native American*

"The spirit, the will to win, and the will to excel are the things that endure." ~ *Vince Lombardi*

19 ~ Leadership

"Real leaders are ordinary people with extraordinary determination." ~ *Source Unknown*

I have a dear friend in my life that I have known since I was six years old. We started off in first grade together. This particular friend is a born leader. Ever since I can remember when it came to electing class presidents, she was the one chosen. She has incredible leadership skills and organizational qualities. This friend has held several jobs and each and every one of them has always been in management. If she doesn't start off with the position, she inevitably ends up with it. If there is anyone who knows how to get a job done, it is her.

Not all people are so lucky that their personalities are so distinctive or apparent. I think the reverse of being a true leader also applies to the characteristics of being a true follower. Both personalities stand out and can more often-than-not be clearly identified. At times; however, being seen as a follower doesn't necessarily endear you to others or even to yourself. Born leaders or take charge people don't always understand or have compassion for those who need to be given more direction and encouragement along the way.

When we don't address our personality type, we could possibly become aggravated when we lose patience with others in our effort to provide guidance.

I also know that there is a grey zone when it comes to these two very different personalities. Nothing is ever that cut and dry in life. I can very much say that I have traits that fall into both zones. You may very well be the same as I think this personality description is far more common than the other two. Some people may even classify the combination of the two opposite personalities as passive-aggressive types. I am not so sure that I agree with this evaluation but it certainly is a popular term these days. However, I do think that by engaging in a real honest self-evaluation, we can decide which category we fall into. In doing so, we can learn to better handle some of the changes we might want to make in our lives. Thus we can become more responsible and accountable for our own happiness.

"In the last analysis, the individual person is responsible for living his own life and for 'finding himself'. If he insists in shifting his responsibility to somebody else, he fails to find out the meaning of his own existence." ~ **Thomas Merton**

As previously stated, there is absolutely nothing wrong with either personality. It all boils down to self-acceptance and mutual respect for each other. We aren't all made from the same mold. Life would be very boring if we were. Therefore, the ultimate goal is to learn to appreciate ourselves for whom we are and to change the things about ourselves that are changeable. It is extremely difficult to alter an innate part of our basic being. We can't expect others to do things our way either. We need all types of personalities to effectively make this world of ours go around.

If you are a follower, the key is to follow the right people. If you are a leader, the key is to lead others in an admirable direction. There is a huge difference between leading people and trying to control or bossing them. The difference is as clear as night and day. If you fall somewhere in between the distinct personalities of a leader or follower, use your God-given talents in both areas as wisely as possible. The best way to deal with all personality types is to realize our own individual make-up, to evaluate what we have to offer in any given situation, and to work toward achieving a common goal for the greater good. We can all achieve our goals if we learn to better work together. Each personality has its inherent advantages and disadvantages. We need each other in order to have a more balanced world. I always try to remind myself that no one can accomplish a whole heck of a lot on their own. Leaders need followers in order to accomplish their desired goal. Followers also need great leaders to emulate in helping to get the job done. Those people that have a balance between the two have their work cut out for them. They must discern when to be a pilot or when to be a passenger. It takes great skill to effectively and efficiently learn when to step in to get the job done or to butt out when it is being done the right way.

"There is no higher service than human service. To work for the common good is the greatest creed." ~ *Albert Schweitzer*

Personal Reflections:

1. Okay…now for a little truth serum. What personality category best suits you? Are you a born leader, a follower, or a combination of the two?
2. If so, do you like yourself in this role? If not, why?
3. To born leaders…when others need too much guidance from you do you get frustrated with them? In other words, do you end up resenting them at times?
4. To born followers…when people try to guide you more than you would like, do you get frustrated with

them? Do you eventually resent them and see them as trying to take control of your life?
5. To those with both capabilities…do you know when to use your leadership qualities and when not to?

20 ~ A New Word to Make You Smile

I heard a new word not so long ago on TV for the very first time. I honestly don't think it's a real word or that you could find it in any dictionary but I really like the sound of it. The word is "smize". Actually it is probably spelled "sm-eyes". I'm not quite sure of the correct spelling but it is actually irrelevant to what I am about to share with you. I merely want to ask if you've ever heard this word before and do you know what it means?

Before I tell you what this TV host said it means, I want to ask you another question. Have you ever heard the expression that the "eyes are the window to the soul"? I love this saying because when I look into people's eyes, I see their spirit. Sometimes, I see kindness, joy, sadness, anger, and so on. I think the eyes really do give away our innermost feelings if we let them. The expression reflected in our eyes can really make us feel quite vulnerable. I think our eyes are our most precious feature and clearly demonstrate our inner beauty if that is what lies there. In fact, I think the eyes are the most expressive physical feature we have and the one I certainly value the most.

Okay, so now back to the meaning of this so-called new word. I gave you a bit of a clue to its meaning when I clarified the spelling. "Sm-eyes" means to "smile with your eyes". I like the meaning of this new word. To me, when our whole face lights up when we smile, is what true "sm-eyesing" is really all about. Several times in my life, I have heard the expression, he or she smiled in such a way but the smile never quite reached their eyes. Does that make sense to you? Have you ever smiled as you look into a mirror? Hey, give it a try. You've got nothing to lose. Have a good look and see what other people see when you smile at them. In other words...do you sm-eyes? The answer to this question is far more important than anyone of us might fully realize.

When I was extrapolating on the meaning of this new word with one of my friends Charles Betts as he shared with me on my blog site. *"I think the word "sm-eyes"...smiling with our eyes and its concept are a beneficial principle to apply to our daily routines. The eyes are for sure a window to the soul. I have known some people in life who have, due to rough circumstances in life, drawn the shades over the windows and refuse to let people see in. From my perspective it appears they feel that if no-one sees in then they are safe. They feel that any intruders are there only to take things from their soul which they do not want to give away or share.*

Their world becomes smaller and tighter and they eventually dry up inside.

When my two daughters were in their formative years and would come home from school, having been hurt or disappointed by their friends, they would express a desire to have nothing to do with that friend. I would say: If you continue to cut off your friends when they hurt you, eventually you will end up in a small circle by yourself". I wanted them to learn that pain will come but we must overcome the pain with love and forgiveness. Love will never dry up as long as we let it flow. Only when we dam it up inside does it dry up.

To get back to the word "sm-eyes", yes...we do benefit when we learn to let our eyes express the beauty of our souls. If someone abuses that beauty then they have some issues in their own soul. They need our friendship and prayers. As does God deal with us, we can be blessed when we love because it is in us, not because someone deserves it. In this way we are in control of our own happiness, not those we deal with. So it is that we "sm-eyes" all those we contact. Both they and we are blessed."

Personal Reflections:

1. This personal reflection is going to be plain and simple. Do you "sm-eyes" and if not, why not?

2. Are you trying to protect yourself by not allowing people to see your sensitive side?
3. Do you like when people "sm-eyes" at you or does it make you feel uncomfortable?

21 ~ Driving Miss "D"

I have formed a very unique friendship with someone I have come to admire and respect. I don't know her full story but I do know that she has experienced a deep loss. She made a decision to overcome that loss by starting a blog. Several years ago our blogging paths crossed and we have become dear friends. I have never met her in person. I only refer to her as Hope. She has come to call me "Miss D". I'm pretty sure I'm old enough to be her mother but she has helped me every bit as much as I hope I have helped her. Hope is one talented girl. She is a beautiful poet and writes great stories to share her talent with the world. Every morning in cyberspace, I visit with her. She doesn't know my full story either but for one reason or another our heart-strings are attached. We found each other because it was meant to be, that I know for sure.

I love the nickname Hope has given me. As you know, my name is **D**olores. Little does Hope know…yet I'm sure she suspects that I have known many other words starting with the letter **D** which have **d**eeply affected me over the years. I know the meaning of **d**iscouragement and **d**isappointment like so many of us have but I also have experienced **d**espair and **d**eep **d**epression. Over thirty years ago, I could hardly convince myself to get out of bed. If it weren't for my young children and the need to get them off to school, I'm not so sure I would have bothered. During those dark times in my life I felt very little hope, if any at all.

I have formed another very unique and precious cyberspace friendship with a woman named Nikki. Nikki and I also communicate on a daily basis. We know a lot more about each other because we have read each other's books and we've had the opportunity apart from the blogging world to share more personal information. Nikki makes my day in much the same way as Hope. She is open and honest. She's had a tough life but she found peace with it by finding her faith. She is a survivor of rape and abuse, both physical and emotional. She has also created a blog to help in her healing process. She has touched my life in such a way that it brings tears to my eyes as I think of her story.

I feel so fortunate to have found such wonderful friends. In the old days, they would be called pen pals. I had one or two of them in my school days but with the technological advances present today, there is no longer the need for paper and pen communication. By reaching out, these two women have honored me in such an indescribable way. We have shared our stories of hope. We have inspired each other in our personal healing journeys. We have learned to trust again and to look on the bright side of things. I personally have found another **D** word which my daughter uses in her writing to describe her relationship with God. I have found the **D**ivine. The One who is all loving and all merciful. The One that loves me no matter what. You know what else? I have discovered several other words beginning with **D** to describe where I am in my journey today. I have encountered a **D**eity that surrounds me with **d**aylight instead of **d**arkness, **d**elight instead of **d**read and **d**espair, and **d**auntless faith instead of **d**eep **d**epression based on irrational fears. I much prefer these words starting with **D** rather than the opposite ones I was previously feeling on a far more regular basis.

Personal Reflections:

1. Have you or do you suffer from some of the same **D** words described in this chapter?
2. If so, do you count on your family and friends to help you rise above your **d**espair, **d**read, or **d**epression?
3. Have you figured out ways to help yourself in order to **d**iscover your faith and **d**elight in the life you have been so richly given?

22 ~ Change

"The best and most beautiful things in the world cannot be seen or even touched. They must be felt with the heart." ~ Helen Keller

As I have already stated several times, I have been married to my husband for over forty-five years. Every night when I pray before I fall asleep, I thank God for this wondrous gift. My husband isn't perfect. Hey…but then, neither am I. However, one of the very first things I am grateful for each and every day and night is our long time marriage and the love and loyalty we share despite the ups and downs of any lifelong commitment. We have experienced financial hardship, job loss, ill physical and emotional health, and other typical marriage woes. Over the years, we have learned the true meaning of our marriage vows. I have discovered that I married my best friend who has stuck by my side through thick and thin. Figuratively speaking…because my husband is not the most demonstrative type of guy, we've held each other's hand as we worked through these trials and tribulations. No one ever said that it was going to be easy but it's been well worth it.

Many years ago when we were in our late teens, my husband's brother tried to influence us not to get married so young. He was eight years older than us and he was offering his younger brother what he thought was some sage advice. Needless to say, we never took it; however, I recall a humorous moment in the first few years of our marriage when my husband showed a little "sass". He mentioned to his brother that "if he had known marriage was going to be this great, he would have gotten married sooner!" So yes…I do have every reason to be grateful for this husband of mine. What about you? Are there things in your life that you are grateful for or don't want to change?

For instance, here is another example of being grateful for the simple things in our lives. Do you have a favorite chair in your home? Do you usually have the tendency to sit in the same kind of chair whenever possible or wherever you go? I know that I do!

When I have the opportunity to visit in other people's homes, one of the first things I do after the initial niceties are out-of-the-way is look for the spot where I am going to sit. I scan the room with hopeful anticipation that I will find a rocking chair or glider rocker. To me, this kind of chair is both comfortable and comforting. In new and awkward situations, when I have the chance to sit on one, it takes the edge off the moment as the rocking motion brings its soothing relief to me.

It is very hard for me to start my day without a short stint on my rocking chair each and every morning. It sets the pace for the whole day as I find my source of peace and contentment in this simplest of ways. It is during this time on my rocking chair that I listen to the softest of music and feel so inspired. This is my time, this is my special spot.

On holidays or visiting with family and friends, I always feel a tiny absence in my life when I'm "off my rocker". I can't be the only one that feels this way. What about you? Do you miss the comfort of your special chair? Are there some things in your life that you just don't want to change?

"You have not found your place until all your faculties are roused, and your whole nature consents and approves of the work you are doing..." ~ *Orison Swett Marden*

23 ~ Live...Laugh...Love ~ More on a Lighter Note

"In the midst of hate, I found there was, within me, an invincible love. In the midst of tears, I found there was, within me, an invincible smile. In the midst of chaos, I found there was, within me, an invincible calm. I realized, through it all, that in the middle of winter, I finally found that within me there lies an invincible summer." ~ Albert Camus

A few years ago, I received an email from my oldest granddaughter. She made me laugh. She was using words like "u" instead of "you" and some of the other shorthand words that young people use today when texting to speed up the process. I remember when she signed off with a colon and a bracket. I had to write her back and ask her what it meant. She told me to look at it by tilting my head to the side and I would see that it was meant to be a smile. Doing just that, actually made me smile. I must admit that I find it so interesting to learn all these new methods of communication. This has encouraged me to make every effort to continue to increase my computer knowledge.

Not too long ago, the only thing I knew how to do was to send or respond to emails and google for information about a subject I wanted to research. I'm still no computer whiz but I'm pretty sure that even my granddaughter would be proud of my progress. The reason I'm mentioning her today is because at the end of an email she sent me, she had signed off with Live…Laugh…Love.

As soon as I saw these closing words, I immediately asked her if she minded if I signed off the same way. She gladly gave me permission and I have utilized this salutation several times when I email my friends or autograph one of my books. Often times, I think of my granddaughter when I do so. Every time I use them in any way, I take the opportunity to ponder upon the true meaning of these three simple little words in hope that the receiver of my message will be richly blessed.

"You will find as you look back upon your life that the moments that stand out, the moments when you have really lived, are the moments when you have done things in the spirit of love." ~ Henry Drummond

Now, after all these years I must admit that I am still not a computer whiz. However, I will say this…I am a very determined person. If I don't know something, I ask someone who does. I've plodded along and figured out an awful lot on my own. I've gained confidence and self-esteem in the process.

The other day, my husband came up from his basement office and admitted to me that he can't believe how far I've come in this regard. It is so neat to hear him compliment me this way. He's always had computer skills far greater than mine, but now, once in a while I can actually educate him on a new skill I've learned on my own. I'm grateful for the support and encouragement that I receive so that I can plod on and educate myself in this new and exciting way.

"All things are difficult before they are easy." ~ Thomas Fuller

In the olden days, we could only communicate with those that lived nearby. In this situation, it was from our lips to their ears. Now with all the advanced technology, one of the best ways to communicate seems to be via computer in one format or another. If it isn't by e-mail, we're logged on to Facebook, Twitter, My Space, chat lines, cell phones, and so on. These methods of communication are all great but have we lost the personal touch? In the future, will we be able to interpret moods, facial expressions, body language, voice intonation, and many other forms of communication, if we choose to mainly communicate the techie way?

Please let us try to remember the personal touch. It's difficult to hug and embrace the "old" way with all the "new" technology. Give someone a smile or a hug today. You'll both feel better for it!

"We cannot rebuild the world ourselves, but we can have a small part in it by beginning where we are. It may only be taking care of a neighbor's child or inviting someone to dinner, but it's important." ~ Donna L. Glazier

24 ~ My Phantom Tooth ~ More on a Lighter Note

"Once you have learned to love, you have learned to live." ~ Source Unknown

Have any of you ever had a root canal? If you have, no fun, right? Many years ago when I was overtired, one of my teeth gave way and I had to go on antibiotics to clear up an abscess and then eventually have a root canal.

The procedure itself wasn't as bad as I thought it would be. What concerned me the most was that the tooth giving me the trouble wasn't a back tooth that could be easily concealed if things didn't go as I hoped. It would be very evident if I lost this tooth.

Over the years, I've had a lot of trouble with this root canal. I had to have it redone about ten years later because it got re-infected. As recently as four years ago it was necessary to have oral surgery to treat it once again. Shortly thereafter, I was forced to have the tooth extracted as the infection reared its ugly head yet again. It seemed that every time I overdid things and let myself get run down this phantom tooth acted up and started to ache. It was almost like a built-in alarm system to remind me to slow down. At last, I'm finally learning how to better listen to this body of mine by being aware of my inner signal, my phantom tooth.

We all have inner guidelines to help us not overdo. Mine just happens to be my missing tooth which somehow or other, can still ache. My dentist tells me that there is now a weakness in this area where a healthy tooth once existed. According to him, this is why I have phantom toothaches.

"Health, Learning & Virtue will ensure your happiness; they will give you a quiet conscience, private esteem & public honor." ~ Thomas Jefferson

Personal Reflections:

1. What is your weakness and how does it manifest itself?
2. What is it trying to tell you?
3. I'm slowly learning to listen to my body. It doesn't mean that I always like what it has to say but I know I should obey. When I don't, I'm the one who pays the price in the end. Can you relate to this?

25 ~ Common Courtesy

"We find greatest joy, not in getting, but in expressing what we are...Men do not really live for honors or for pay; their gladness is not in the taking and holding, but in the doing, the striving, the building, the living. It is a higher joy to teach than to be taught. It is good to get justice, but better to do it; fun to have things but more to make them. The happy man is he who lives the life of love, not for the honors it may bring, but for life itself." ~ R. J. Baughan

"Courteous people learn courtesy from the discourteous." ~ Laura Fitzgerald

Does this quote from the book *Veil of Roses* by Laura Fitzgerald ring a bell with you or make any sense to you? It sure does to me. Common courtesy or common decency can be as uncommon as common sense. As you can see, I'm full of oxymorons as I take the opportunity to elaborate on this subject. What I am actually trying to say is this...when I witness people being rude or unkind to others, it really gets my goat. As soon as I observe such unacceptable behavior I always do a self-check. Subsequently, I almost bend over backwards to treat people with even more kindness than I normally do.

There is no way that I want to behave in such a discourteous or disrespectful manner. In essence, I immediately become even more courteous and behave the exact opposite of the negative behavior that I may have just observed. Therefore, the above quote may actually be true in many instances. If people are discourteous in your presence, it may have a positive impact on your future behavior. My husband and I have a couple of cute expressions of our own. When we observe bad behavior my husband will often say…"if I ever act like that, please let me know" or "remind me 'not' to act in such a rude manner". What do you think? Do you also bend over backwards to 'not' act the same discourteous way that you may have witnessed?

I had a very rewarding conversation with one of my daughters a few years ago. At the end of the school year, my granddaughters were receiving their final report cards. This was an especially important end-of-the-year ceremony because they were in the process of moving to another city during the summer. My two oldest granddaughters were fifteen and twelve at the time and it created a period of adjustment for them. Although, my daughter realized that there would be a transition period, she had every reason to be optimistic. Both girls were doing well in school and had received academic awards in the past. At the finale of this particular year-end ceremonies, the younger granddaughter received this very unique award. It was titled the **WWJD** Award.

I reacted the very same way as my daughter did when she first heard the news that Becca was to receive this special award. I quickly asked, "What in the world does **WWJD** stand for"? This was her reply…"It stands for the "**W**hat **W**ould **J**esus **D**o" Award if He were in your shoes.

In essence, my granddaughter's classmates had nominated her for the award in recognition of the most Christ-like behavior observed by them in her interactions with her peer group. That sounds like a fine compliment to me. Wouldn't it be wonderful if our behavior emulated Christ's as well in our dealings with our own peer group?

On a similar note, sometime ago, my then two-year old granddaughter told me that I was her best friend. Wow…where does a two-year old hear such an expression? Well, she has three older siblings and I'm sure she heard it from one of them when they were talking either with or about their friends.

I was very touched when she made this comment, although, I'm not so sure she knew exactly what she was saying. Young children, usually go to great lengths and have much need for a best friend. It's all part of the growing up process. I'm pretty sure we have all been there.

As the years have gone by, I've come to realize that my younger girlish need for a best friend no longer exists. My best friend is my husband and all my female and male friends are just that, my friends. I love them, enjoy them, and I relish the relationships that we share.

Over the years as part of the maturation process, I have changed my focus. For many years now, my goal in life has been "to be" a best friend rather than "to have" a best friend based on some insecure need of mine. By doing so, I hope my aspiration of emulating my granddaughter in her **WWJD** behavior shines out as much as humanly possible. I have surrounded myself with a wonderful group of people, both female and male. I always try my best to be a true and loyal friend. I have every desire to take their feelings into consideration at every opportunity. Hopefully, one day my young granddaughter will realize that I am truly her best friend because I love her with all my heart. Isn't that what being a best friend is really all about? I sure hope so because my friends mean the world to me.

As I continue on this lighter note, I would like to add that I try to view life in the simplest of ways and to use my imagination as much as possible to explain my thoughts. This is the reason I use my personal experiences to make a variety of points. It is necessary for me to draw from this wealth of information in order to urge you to tap into your past and find the correlation between your life and what I am trying to say. This gives my readers a better chance of relating to my message and how it might apply in their own lives.

Here's another example of tapping into your imagination. Our lives can be as plain and simple as two slices of bread stuck together with butter or as exciting as the ingredients that we put into it. I much prefer what is between the slices of bread rather than the bread itself, although, I do enjoy good quality bread. In reality, I need both.

I want my sandwich so thick with meat and other fixings so that I can hardly wrap my mouth around it. This is the same way that I want to enjoy my life. I don't just want to be born and then eventually die. That's a given. In other words, I don't merely want to exist. I want a lot of in-between stuff to make a really good life for myself and for those around me.

I can settle for bread squeezed together with butter or margarine or I can have a huge "Dagwood" sandwich with all of my favorite things in the middle. It's up to me. As I said, I can settle for less or build my life in much the same way that

I make my sandwiches, thick with messy and juicy flavors like pickles and peppers. I want to lead a full and rewarding life that is pleasing to my Maker. How about you? Would you be a possible candidate for the **WWJD** Award?

26 ~ What's Eating Gilbert Grape?

"An obvious fact about negative feelings is often overlooked. They are caused by us, not by exterior happenings. An outside event presents the challenge, but we react to it. So we must attend to the way we take things, not to the things themselves." ~ Vernon Howard

My daughter uses a neat expression when she notices that someone doesn't appear to be up to snuff or in a particularly good mood. She will say, "I wonder what's eating Gilbert Grape!" Sometimes I feel like Gilbert Grape myself. For whatever reason, I occasionally get set off by the negative behavior of others just like we all do. I am going to explain one of my pet peeves to you. Maybe it's one of yours too.

First of all I want to start by asking a question. In your opinion, is there such a concept as "reasonable" expectations? If not, this chapter probably does not apply to...if so, please read on. At times, I get frustrated by what appears to be a lack of response or reaction to a request I've made or a question I've asked. Let me put it another way. Am I being unreasonable if I ask a question and expect an answer? I will give you a few other examples of what I mean even if they don't all apply to you just so that you get a better understanding of the point I am trying to make. Some may apply while others may not. These are simply yes and no types of questions...

If someone gives you their word...is it reasonable to expect them to keep it?

If you send an email asking a question or questions ....is it reasonable to expect a response?

If you leave a message on someone's answering machine...is it reasonable to expect them to return your call?

If you celebrate a person's birthday with a card, gift, or treat them to lunch...is it reasonable to expect them to acknowledge your birthday in some way, shape, or form?

If you have gone out of your way to help a person out (i.e. by helping them move for instance)....is it reasonable to expect that they might return a similar favor one day should you require their help?

When a friend's been sick and you've supported them by sending cards or gifts...is it reasonable to think they might wish you well when you're ill or at least call to see how you are doing?

These are just examples of a few possible questions I am using in order to make my point. I would love to know if you can identify with it. Do you ever have "reasonable" expectations? Or in other words, are you disappointed when others don't react the way you think they might considering the friendship you have or the relationship you might have formed? If so...does that mean it is wrong to feel the way you do?

I am making every effort to have fewer expectations of people. Trust me, this is no easy endeavor. I am working very hard to turn that occasional sour grape attitude of mine into a reason to celebrate. I am also making every effort to dwell on the positives in my life and be grateful for all my blessings. We all have bad days when people turn us off and we get these negative emotions that certainly don't make us feel any better about the person or the situation.

What can we do about it? We can change our own attitudes just like it was stated in the previous quote by Vernon Howard and not fall into the negative claptrap. It is not easy to be in a positive frame of mind all of the time but when we work at it, it can really make a big difference. Most of us have heard the adage about being handed a lemon in life and turning it into lemonade. Well, we all know what we can turn grapes into...right? Celebrate the good things in your life and more good things will come your way. Cheers to you all!

Personal Reflections:
1. Is it okay to have "reasonable" expectations of others? If so, why? If not, why? Please Note: There are pros and cons to both answers. Do you know what they are?
2. Is it okay to admit to yourself that someone's behavior has negatively affected you?
3. When a family member or friend is not there for you when you've been there for them in the past, how do you react?
4. Do you have the ability and wherewithal to turn the situation around and respond in a positive manner?

27 ~ Self-Acceptance and Regrets

How many of us live without regrets? No one...I am sure! How many of us repeat the same mistakes over and over again? If we don't learn from our mistakes, this is exactly what we will do. Often times, I will ask myself the rhetorical question of why a certain situation arises over and over again in my life. My daughter's answer is that I didn't learn my lesson the first time around.

When history repeats itself, even if the players are different, I try to remember my daughter's sage words. When a similar situation keeps revisiting me, I have no choice but to acknowledge and accept that there is a life lesson in it for me. It's up to me to figure out what it is and perhaps I will have fewer regrets and more learning power. The gift of wisdom...it can be so elusive.

"Never mistake knowledge for wisdom. One helps you make a living; the other helps you make a life." ~ Sandra Carey

Isn't it strange how we meet many people in life who appear to be so self-confident and poised? Perhaps those who genuinely are, have no need to read motivational books like mine. Maybe, you are one of these fortunate people but the fact that you are at the final stages of reading my book leads me to believe that you might be relating to some of my observations and insights. Many of us are able to project an aura or image that implies that we are more confident than we may actually be.

For those of you who may, at times, feel inadequate, insecure, know the meaning of fear, failure, and human weakness, then perhaps some of what I have to share may very well appeal to you. I sure hope so because this has been my goal all along. I want to reach out and touch people in such an intimate way in order to make a difference in their lives.

Part of this goal is to reassure you that you are not alone and it is okay to be human. We are not all cut from the same cloth and we must make the best of the gifts that we have been so generously given. In my opinion, it is wiser to deal with negative feelings in order to help overcome them so as to better cope with life rather than bury them deep within ourselves. When we suppress our true emotions, sooner or later, they come back to haunt us. Self-acceptance is the key. Although we are equally loved by our Maker, for reasons unknown to us, we are not all equally endowed.

Some stars in the heavenly sky are bigger and brighter than other ones just like the personalities and varied talents of people. When the smaller stars join together they can create the same dazzling effect as some of the larger ones. Some of us need to surround ourselves with like-minded people in order to shine brighter. It's just the way it is. Whether big or small, we all draw our Light from the same Divine Source.

Those of us that may not have the success, confidence, intelligence, good looks, poise etc., that we might desire can benefit from combining what we have to offer with others. In doing so, we can creatively connect to each other to develop our own Milky Way effect. When shining this way we have agreed to cast the light on others in this wonderful and generous way by lighting up the lives of others while simultaneously lighting up our own lives. No candle ever goes out when it lights up another one. It merely succeeds in sharing its fire. It's up to us to share the limelight so that each of us has the opportunity to showcase our talents.

Personal Reflections:

1. Do you like to be in the limelight or the center of attention?
2. If so why? Is it really because you are secure in who you are or in actuality is it the exact opposite?
3. If you prefer to be on the sidelines, do you consider this to be a character flaw? If so, why?

4. Not all personalities like to draw attention to themselves. I've asked this question before, do you consider yourself to be an introvert or an extrovert?
5. Do you accept yourself for whom you are or do you secretly wish you were more like someone else? Please Note: It is okay to want to emulate others but it is also necessary to positively embrace our own personalities. There is no benefit in coveting another person's life and being dissatisfied with our own.

28 ~ And the Winner is...Not Me!

One of my husband's favorite lines is, "it's hard to fly like an eagle when you're surrounded by a bunch of turkeys". ~ *Source Unknown*

I previously mentioned in one of my other chapters, The Weather Channel, that my husband should consider being a sit-down-comedian. He certainly has the makings of one as he comes up with some pretty humorous comments from what appears to be an endless supply of quips. In jest, he used to say the above quote quite often during his working years to express his frustration when dealing with the shortcomings of people. I can't help but wonder what they were saying about him.

After publishing my first book, my husband persuaded me to enter a book writing contest. My initial response was "no way". First of all, I never realized that you had to actually submit a fee to enter this particular contest and possibly other ones as well. There were other necessary procedures and requirements that were needed along with this submission entry fee. Up to this point, I was naïve enough to think that people actually nominated authors to be selected as a potential winners in writing contests based on the pleasure they found in reading their books. It never entered my mind that writers paid a fee to submit their own books. Also the other reason I was reluctant to enter this contest is that I only had one book under my belt and I knew there was a lot of room for improvement. My husband rationalized that if I didn't enter then there was no way I could win. Therefore, even if it was a long shot I entered the contest with major reservations and against my better judgment. Internally, I didn't want the negative feelings of realizing that my book wasn't up to par.

You guessed it! I did not win.

Since then, I have heard and read several comments to the effect that merely having written a book makes us all winners. It has been said that there were no losers in this contest because we have accomplished a great feat by having the courage to enter our books in the contest. Well, yes and no. This rationalization does not totally make sense or even appeal to me. It sounds more like an appeasement. Why enter a contest in the first place if there is no honor or reward in winning it? If we are all winners even if we lose, than maybe the reverse is true and the winners are losers too just like the rest of us.

Whoever said, 'It's not whether you win or lose that counts,' probably lost." ~ Martina Navratilova

I'm Not Perfect And It's Okay is written in an imperfect way much like its author, me. I'm sorry to admit that there are a few typos in it that my editor, my proofreaders and I missed. Oops...I guess they are not perfect either. I heard an expression just the other day. It was about being "beautifully imperfect". I've now made that my own personal goal, to be beautiful despite my imperfections.

However, in the end, it is my name on my book and I am ultimately responsible for its content. I wouldn't have it any other way. Yes, maybe it is not as well-written or as polished as some other books, but what the heck; I gave it my best shot. The negative consequence of not winning the contest will not deter me. It will only suffice to make me more determined. I'm like a dog with a bone and I'm not going to give up that easy.

Although, I will say this...no matter how hard anyone may try to flower up the facts, to be brutally honest, along with many other authors...I lost and some other authors won. That's a fact. Contests are actually competitions. In most, if not all competitive events, there are winners and losers. Usually, there are far more losers than winners. I will not take that honor away from the winners. By saying that we are all winners in this book writing contest does just that....it takes away from the winners. I lost, I know it, and I'm not afraid to admit it. I'm not afraid to admit this either. It mattered…in fact, it mattered a lot more than I thought it would. I have a competitive spirit and it's no fun to lose. I'm sure that it mattered to the winners too. If it didn't, why would any of us enter contests in the first place?

Therefore, on that note I would like to congratulate all the winners in, not only writing contests, but in other competitive events as well. It feels so wonderful to win and hopefully one day the rest of us will win a contest too. There is nothing wrong with being a gracious loser or gracious winner for that matter either.

"Do not go where the path may lead you, go instead where there is no path and leave a trail." ~ Ralph Waldo Emerson

This is a very profound quote. If I can leave anything with you today, I would like to give you the gift of believing in yourself. It won't happen in one day, but maybe it will be the first seed that when nurtured, will bloom into a very fruitful tree. So many of us look for validation outside of ourselves to identify who we are by how others react to us. We may look to others for approval instead of being our authentic self. It is necessary to find that validation from within in order to have a true belief in ourselves.

If we rely on others to form this belief, we may lose sight of all that we hope to be because we have compromised facets of our own personality and character so that we will be loved and accepted. This is conditional love. It takes real courage and true grit to be different and stand up for our beliefs. We can only find this courage when we have the strength and determination to validate who we are from the inner stirrings of our Maker.

Although, these stirrings may begin by a dissatisfaction or lack of contentment in our lives that just won't leave us, there is a reason for this. If we are always satisfied with our situation in life, there would be no room for growth or any desire to change our circumstances or anyone else's for that matter. Growth results in many fine attributes like self-worth, self-esteem, and a desire to make a difference. With these attributes, we learn about hope and the gift of believing in ourselves…a gift so wondrous that we can stand tall and be exactly whom we were meant to be regardless of other people's opinion of us.

Be true to these inner stirrings and you will learn how to believe in yourself.

When I look at all the great authors in my writing and reading path, I know that I am in great company. I feel like I am soaring with eagles and not "surrounded by a bunch of turkeys". We are a bunch of gifted writers making a difference by sharing our God-given talents.

"Achievement is not always success, while reputed failure often is. It is honest endeavor, persistent effort to do the best possible under any and all circumstances." ~ Orison Swett Marden

Personal Reflections:

1. Do you ever enter contests? If so what kind and do you hope to win?
2. Do you enter personal ones that have the opportunity to evaluate your talent?
3. If you don't win, how do you feel about it?
4. If you do win, does it make sense to you if someone says…everyone is a winner in this contest just because they entered it? Four of my grandchildren play hockey and some of the other grandchildren play different sports. When anyone of them loses their game, even at their young age, I have yet to hear them say that even though they lost the game…"they still won".

29 ~ Extraordinarily Ordinary

"There are no great people in this world, only great challenges which ordinary people rise up to meet." ~ William Frederick Halsy, Jr.

Over forty years ago, my niece Lori was born. When she came into this world, it was a milestone birth for me because I was given the first-time honor of becoming a Godmother to this lovely little baby. In most instances, one might consider being a Godparent as a pretty ordinary thing but to me it was really quite extraordinary. In my day, it usually meant that if the parents were unable to care for the child, the Godparent would be willing to take on this huge responsibility in the parent's absence. Nowadays, I'm pretty sure most parents have guardians named in their Wills if the need should arise but I'm not so sure that was as prevalent in my younger years, at least not to my knowledge. We took a lot more for granted and had the tendency to assume that our children would be taken care of by our chosen family members if the unthinkable should happen.

We later honored our siblings in much the same way when our children were born. We chose carefully in order to ensure that if the need ever arose, our children would be loved and provided for in much the same way as we would raise them ourselves.

As the years went by we were given the honor of becoming Godparents on more than one occasion. Each and every time it felt like such an extraordinary event. It was always a great honor to be selected. Now all these years later, although we don't have the same initial responsibility of taking over for the parents if need be, I feel we still have the responsibility of setting an example for these wonderful Godchildren. This makes our role in their lives still extraordinary even to this day. I'm grateful to have had this opportunity and to be honored in this way.

"Each time the world needs an extra touch of love and gentle caring, God creates a Godmother." ~ Source Unknown

30 ~ Savor the Flavor

I received a lovely Christmas present from a gentleman in his mid-seventies whom I hardly know. He is actually a dear and longtime friend of my sister.

I feel that a great gift has been bestowed upon me at this later stage of my life in what I refer to as the beginning of my twilight years. After completion of my first book *I'm Not Perfect and It's Okay*, I found such wonderful support from my husband, my family and my friends. This, too, felt like a generous gift which created that Christmas feeling all year long.

The gentleman I mentioned earlier became a fan of mine shortly after he read my first book. On completion of reading it, he demonstrated a keen desire to read more. He eagerly accepted to read the manuscript for my second book. Are you like me? Do you like immediate feedback? Do you patiently wait to hear or read the reactions of others to what you have so carefully written? Our words are so important to us because they are an expression of our innermost self that we are choosing to share with others. This choice involves risk. I feel I show my faith the most when I am prepared to take that risk. By choosing to share my words with you today

I am taking a small step in my life journey in order to grow in faith.

On Christmas Eve, shortly before my sister's friend was to attend Midnight Mass, he gave me the most incredible Christmas gift. I had sent him my second manuscript a few weeks earlier and was waiting patiently to get some feedback. He wrote that he was reading the chapter titled God's Wife and he was so moved by it that he decided to immediately e-mail me. He mentioned that he was reading my manuscript much like he was enjoying Christmas candy. He was reading slowly to better absorb and digest my words and their meaning. He said that he was enjoying what I had written in the way that I meant it to be read…slowly, very slowly, one chapter at a time to "savor the flavor".

I think that is an excellent expression to describe my inspirational books and the Christmas Season as well. The true meaning of Christmas is meant to be savored all year long because it is the gift that keeps on giving. Savor the flavor…sounds like a fine compliment to me. What wonderful gifts God has in store for us all! It is so enchanting to discover a new talent later on in life. It means we still have room for growth and more opportunities to reveal our hidden talents.

Personal Reflections:

1. Do you consider yourself to be a talented person?
2. If so, do you think you have discovered all your talents or are you open to uncovering some latent possibilities?
3. Have you tapped into to any other resources to help zero in on your creative abilities in another direction?

Conclusion

I have learned that success is to be measured not so much by the position one has reached in life as by the obstacles which he has overcome in trying to succeed." ~ **Booker T. Washington**

The majority of my writing is faith-based and I draw from my own personal inspiration and relationship with God. I don't know the plan. All I know is that I am...as are you, part of the Divine Plan which is far greater than anyone of us could possibly imagine. If things don't go quite as we expect or see fit, it doesn't mean to say that all won't turn out for the better. Miracles take time.

Often times, life can appear magical but miracles don't happen quite as quickly. We must exercise extreme patience and diligence in order for our own personal plan to unfold. God is not in a hurry nor should we be.

"The sculptor will chip off all unnecessary material to set the angel free. Nature will chip and pound us remorselessly to bring out our possibilities. She will strip us of wealth, humble our pride, humiliate our ambition, let us down from the ladder of fame, will discipline us in a

thousand ways, if she can develop a little character. Everything must give way to that. Wealth is nothing, position is nothing, fame is nothing, and manhood is everything." ~ Orison Swett Marden

Good things can and do happen to good people. God has promised us many things and He is true to His Word. We must count on that in our daily lives.

"Each experience through which we pass operates ultimately for our good...This is a correct attitude to adopt...and we must be able to see it in that light." ~ Raymond Holliwell

We don't always recognize the work of God, but if we are patient with ourselves and take the time to reflect, we will create the opportunity to see exactly how God works. When we do, we will be forever grateful and recognize how truly blessed we are.

Bonus Chapter
A Woman's Voice ~ Volume 2

1 ~ The Inception of A Woman's Voice

"Remember no one can make you feel inferior without your consent." ~ *Eleanor Roosevelt*

I recently had a lovely conversation with one of my twin daughters. A few years ago, she had the wonderful occasion to attend a conference in Los Angeles, California. I could clearly hear the enthusiasm and pleasure in her voice as she described her experience to me. This was a conference for women and by women. Attendees varied in ages from, twenty-something, to a woman in her eighties. They all had a common goal…they wanted to find their voices and learn to better express themselves. In other words, they all desired the same end goal. These women wanted to be "heard".

Before I share a small part of her experience with you, I want to relate to you how she heard about this special event in the first place. My daughter is a social worker who has been a stay-at-home mother for the last several years. She has had four children in a ten year span and they keep her challenged and extremely busy. She has chosen to put her career on hold in order to meet the ever growing demands of her little family.

Before this particular conference, her husband sent her the information via e-mail giving her the heads up about this event specifically geared for women knowing that it would be of great interest to her. I chuckled to myself when my daughter told me she emailed her husband back at work. She asked him…"why would he send this information to her when he knew full well that she would be unable to attend" due to her busy home life and domestic demands. Guess what happened next? Her husband must have secretly wanted her to go because he helped make it happen. He took on the responsibilities of their young family for almost five days so that my daughter could benefit from this learning opportunity. She was about to experience a first time adventure by getting away alone to enjoy a totally new and exciting experience.

The presenter of the conference was speaking on this particular topic (women's voices) for the first time. Therefore, my daughter was part of the inception stage of this relevant topic by the organizer of the conference. Approximately five hundred women from all over Canada and the United States attended. In a nutshell, the theme of the conference was about the voices of women and the desire to be heard. My daughter was given this great opportunity because her husband made the choice to instinctually hear her voice and helped create the occasion for her to meet with other women in their efforts to also be heard. In my opinion, my daughter actually already had a voice at home because her husband was instrumental in getting her to conference. It was apparent to me that no matter what your walk of life may be, you can have the opportunity to have a voice. In other words, that voice starts in the home. Once it is heard there it can evolve into other forums as well.

Shortly thereafter, my daughter returned home a much more enlightened and contented individual. The fire was burning strong inside her with the keen desire to make a difference in this oftentimes, troubled world, we call home. Her enthusiasm lit my fire too! Yes...we all have a voice and we all want to be heard. Now, the real challenge is yet to unfold as we make every effort to find someone who is willing to listen. We often hear the expression that someone is a "gifted speaker". I have a sneaking suspicion that the seldom...if ever used expression..."gifted listener", is equally common or viewed as equally important. Trust me...it is!

"Don't compromise yourself. You are all you've got."
~ Betty Ford

"If better is possible, good is not enough." ~ Source Unknown

Personal Reflections:
1. Do you consider yourself to have a voice in either the work place or at home?
2. If so, are you communicating effectively and truly expressing yourself as an equal when you have the opportunity to speak?
3. Do you have the tendency to voice your opinion only when it agrees with strong-minded individuals or do you feel strong enough in your own views to publicly disagree with others? Hint: A good example of not feeling comfortable with your views is having the tendency to discuss them afterwards with a friend or co-worker whom you know will agree with you and your take on things.

TO CONTACT AUTHOR:

WEBSITE

http://www.doloresayotte.com

BLOG SITE

http://www.doloresayotte.wordpress.com

FACEBOOK AUTHOR'S PAGE

http://www.facebook.com/Author.Dolores.Ayotte

www.ingramcontent.com/pod-product-compliance
Lightning Source LLC
Chambersburg PA
CBHW071512040426
42444CB00008B/1610